Constructive Living for Young People

David K. Reynolds, Ph.D.

2013

Introduction

This book is about the problems of young people today. When you have a problem, whom do you ask for advice? Your friends? Your parents? Your teachers? Maybe you can find advice in magazines or in books or on television or on the radio or on the Internet. In this book you will find some answers to problems facing young people today. They are not the only possible answers. They are not the absolute, final answers. The advice in this book is based on my experience with young people and with Constructive Living. Please think about this advice and discuss it with your family and schoolmates and teachers. Find your own solutions to the problems you face. I hope this book will be useful for discovering your best path from childhood to young adulthood.

Here are some questions young people ask me. It doesn't matter whether the young people are

Japanese or American. Their questions are quite similar. And my answers are not just for Japanese teenagers or for American teenagers. My answers are for young people anywhere. Please think about them.

Questions and Answers

Question 1: The students in my class don't invite me to go with them anywhere. I feel left out. I feel isolated from the group. What can I do to make them include me in their activities? How can I have more friends?

Feeling isolated and lonely is unpleasant for anyone, especially when others around you seem to have lots of friends. It isn't useful just to sit and think about how unhappy you are. Your feelings of unhappiness are natural. They arise naturally from your situation. Don't fight with the feelings. Don't try to pretend you don't care about the group. Focusing on your feelings won't solve the problem. Let's consider what you can do to change the situation. If you sit and wait for friends to come to you, you may wait a long time. So let's try a more active approach.

Are there other classmates who seem to be alone a lot? Are there new classmates who have no friends yet? Are there classmates who are ill and unable to come to school? Are there classmates with physical handicaps? You could offer to study with these classmates. You could offer to walk home with them. You could invite them to visit your home. You could invite them to visit a fast-food restaurant. You could offer to help them with some problem they have.

Perhaps you feel shy to do these things. Perhaps you worry what your classmate will think if you offer to do these things. It's fine to be shy and to worry about what your classmate will think. Your shyness and worry are natural. They reflect your desire to be liked; you don't want to do something foolish or embarrassing. So while being shy, while worrying, invite your classmate to do something with you.

You can't make your feelings change just by wishing they would change. You can't make your classmate accept your invitation either. Feelings are uncontrollable by your will. Classmates and parents and teachers and everybody else are uncontrollable by your will. So is the weather. So are traffic lights. So are the prices of sandwiches and fruit drinks. There are many things in the world that you can't control by your will.

The one thing that you can control by your will is your own behavior. You can control what you do. Even if you are shy or timid or afraid you can control what you do. So you can invite a classmate to do something together even if you are afraid. Inviting is behavior.

Perhaps the classmate will accept your invitation. That's fine. Perhaps the classmate will refuse. That's all right, too. Remember, you can't control what your classmate will do, but you can control what you do. So ask another time or ask another classmate. See what happens. To actively invite others is much more interesting than passively sitting and waiting for them to invite you. Of course, it may be scary to be more active. They may refuse. But you won't die from their refusal. They may accept. Then you may be making a new friend. You may be starting a new group. Inviting is a very small risk because nearly everyone likes to be invited.

When you have a few friends of your own your classmates may think you are popular. They may invite you into other groups, too. Then it is your turn to decide whether to join the other groups or not. You don't have to join. Your behavior is under your own control. Joining is behavior.

Always think clearly about what is controllable and what is not controllable in life. Use your energy on what is controllable, your own behavior, and don't waste your energy trying to fight what is not controllable. Your feelings are uncontrollable. Accept them as they are and go on with your life.

Question 2: When my classmates ask me to do them a favor, I can't refuse. Even if I don't want to do it, I can't refuse. How can I become stronger?

It is natural to want to do a favor for others. You want your classmates to like you. You don't want your classmates to be angry at you. You don't want your classmates to be disappointed in you. But you can say "no." Saying "no" is behavior. Behavior is controllable. Even when you feel weak you can refuse.

I suggest that you use the word "can't" (*dekimasen*, in Japanese) for behaviors that are truly impossible for you. For example, I can't jump to the roof of this building. I can't touch my tongue to my elbow. I can't buy Mt. Everest. However, I can speak in front of a large audience (even though I feel shy). I can ask someone to study with me (even though they might refuse). I can wash windows (even though I don't like to do that work). And I can refuse to do a favor for a classmate (even though I feel weak or frightened).

If you use the word "can't" (*dekimasen*) too much you may mistakenly believe that some possible behavior is impossible. Instead of "I can't do it" please use "I don't want to do it," "I am afraid to do it," "I have never done it," "I dislike doing it," and other substitutes. These substitutes are more honest, and they keep open the possibility that you can do it.

To refuse your classmates' demands does not require strength or courage or any other feeling. Just do it. Be worried and scared and weak and just refuse. That is the path to becoming a mature adult. The next step is to move on quickly to some other topic. Shifting attention to the next thing that needs doing makes your refusal less noticeable.

Question 3: I am overweight. I worry about being fat and ugly. Then my worrying makes

me want to eat. Then I become fatter. What should I do?

Are you really overweight? If you watch television and movies and magazine ads you will see many very slim people. These models and stars aren't typical or normal. Some of them aren't healthy. They are the current fashion. Many young people try to imitate these models of fashion. The young people try to be very slim and wear the same hairstyles and clothes and so forth. So it is important to get an objective measure of your weight.

How much do you weigh? Use scales to measure your weight. What is the normal range of weight for your age and sex and body type? If you are within that range of weight then you are not overweight. If you are heavier than that normal range then you are overweight. It is good for you to be worried about your weight if you are overweight. Being fat is both unfashionable and unhealthy.

The way to lose weight is clear: eat fewer calories and exercise more. There is no magical way to lose weight instantly. If you must lose a lot of fat to bring your weight into the normal range you should talk with your doctor about diet and exercise. Maybe you don't like to do exercise such as aerobics, sports, or even walking. It's not necessary to like exercise. Do it anyway. Remember that your purpose is to lose weight. Then dress properly for the exercise with the proper shoes and other exercise clothing, and do the exercise.

Maybe worrying about being fat makes you hungry. Worrying is fine. Being hungry is fine. Eating too much is not fine. You can't directly control the worry in your mind. You can't directly control the hunger you feel. However, you can control whether you eat and how much you eat. Eating is a behavior. Eating behavior is controllable. When you want to eat between meals try going for a walk instead. Get your body away from food. Or distract yourself by cleaning your room or washing a car or working on a hobby.

It isn't necessary to fight against your worries or your hunger. The more you fight against them, the more you think about them. The more you think about them, the more trouble they are. Just leave the worrying and hunger as they are. Just go on about your life. As time passes you will forget them.

Question 4: I have a problem with alcohol. Recently I drank too much at a party and fell off my motorbike on the way home. Sometimes I drink alcohol before going to school in the morning. How can I overcome my drinking problem?

Wishing your alcohol problem would change won't change it. Talking about your alcohol problem won't change it. The only way to solve your alcohol problem is to stop drinking alcohol. Here are some tips to make it easier to stop drinking alcohol.

First, make it harder to get your hands on alcohol. Don't keep bottles or cans handy. Throw away the ones you have or put them far away in an inconvenient place. If you feel like having a drink you must go to a lot of trouble to get to the alcohol. Sometimes it will be too much trouble.   When you don't drink alcohol you are just like other non-drinkers. You only have an alcohol problem when you are drinking it.

Beware of labels. We are all changeable. In the moments when you don't drink alcohol you are not alcoholic. In the moments when you do drink it you have a momentary problem. There is no permanent problem. So change may be easier than you think.

The next suggestion is to hang out with friends who don't drink alcohol. When your friends are drinking it is harder for you to refuse. If you have a friend who also drinks alcohol ask him or her to make a pact, a promise, to give up alcohol with you. Then you both will support each other in becoming alcohol-free.

Next, it is a good idea to write down the cost of alcohol in your life until now. Begin by calculating, in detail, the amount of money you have spent on alcohol. Then write down the cost of alcohol in terms of your problems with friends, your problems at school, problems with your parents, problems with the law, and so forth. Look clearly at the problems you caused with your drinking. Alcohol itself is not the problem. Your drinking alcohol is the problem. The good news is that you can solve the problem.

Finally, have something else to do when you feel the urge to drink alcohol. Distract yourself with sports or hobbies or texting a friend, anything that takes you away from the place where alcohol is located. You will find that it is easier to distract yourself with activities that move your body. For example, it may be easier to go for a walk or go out shopping than it is to sit and read a book.

Question 5: I become very nervous before taking an exam. Sometimes I feel dizzy just before an exam, and my stomach hurts. Later, when I learn that I did well on the exam, my dizziness and pain go away. Am I crazy?

You are not crazy. You want to do well on the exam so you feel the way you do. Students who don't care how they do on the exam don't have these problems. So your dizziness and stomach problems tell us about your good wishes for success.

The more you fight against your psychosomatic problems and the more you criticize yourself for having them, the stronger they become. So my advice is to accept them as indicators of your strong and positive desire to do well. Then get on with studying for the exam. You might try some distracting sports exercise or relaxation exercise or even thanking the dizziness for its message about your good intentions to do well. However, the main course is to keep on doing what is controllable, studying for the exam. Over the years you will see that the dizziness and pain go away after the exams again and again. When your life experience shows you that these problems are only temporary they will become less troublesome.

Question 6: I feel shy when talking with other students. Especially when I'm at parties or when I'm around young people I don't know well, I can't think of anything to say. I'm afraid I'll say something stupid or embarrassing. After the conversation has moved to another topic I think of something to say about the old topic. My mind works too slowly because I'm so nervous. How can I be more comfortable socially?

You want other people to like you. You don't want to make social mistakes. You want people to think you are clever and up-to-date on current topics. All those desires are normal. As you grow older you will learn that your other classmates want the same thing. Some of them are just as worried as you are about social skills. However, like you, they try not to show their shyness, and you don't notice it because your attention is on your own problem.

The way to overcome your shyness is to focus your attention on other people. Your problems arise because you are so focused on yourself, your own shyness, that you become stiff and unresponsive. When you learn to lose yourself in the conversation or other activity, then you will naturally come up with timely conversation.

Try asking questions to other students and listening carefully to their answers. Without being pushy try to learn about others. Praise them for their good attitudes and behaviors. Don't criticize yourself or others until you gain more self-confidence. Self-confidence will grow as you have more success. First comes success; then comes self-confidence. You cannot generate self-confidence out of nothing, just by thinking about it or wishing for it.

The more you worry, the more you stay home alone to avoid social situations, the more you criticize yourself for your shyness, the more you complain to others about your problems, then the greater your misery. So, while feeling uncomfortable, join social groups or go out with special friends. Shopping, sports events, volunteer activities, and trips provide opportunities to get your attention outside of yourself. The secret for overcoming your shyness is where you place your attention.

Question 7: If I'm not busy all the time I feel guilty. Sometimes my friends just lie around listening to records or talking. I think I must study all the time or I feel restless. How can I learn to relax a little more?

You want to do well in school. Your parents want you to do well in school. So you study long and hard. You can be a better student by developing a well-rounded life. Well-rounded students have better health for studying. They have wider life experiences to understand their study material. So you can become a better student by including some physical exercise and recreation into your daily activities.

You can enjoy your life more without being lazy. Listening to music or playing games or talking with friends can help you become a more skillful human and a better student. Of course, studying is important, too. You must not allow relaxing to become a complete substitute for studying. Being well rounded includes both work and play. So, keeping in mind your purpose to do well in school, enjoy yourself sometimes.

Question 8: My father died suddenly about six months ago. I still feel depressed. How long will

it take to get over these feelings of grief?

There is no set time limit for grieving. Naturally, the grief will fade over time. If you try to make it go away directly you will restimulate it. Grief, like any feeling, is uncontrollable directly by your will. However, there are things you can do to help you get on with life, even while feeling sad sometimes. First, make sure you have done what you need to do about your father's death. Go to his gravesite (or *butsudan* or *kamidana* in Japan) and thank him for specific things he did for you while he was alive. Then tell him goodbye with the hope that his spirit will watch over you.

Make sure that your father's belongings are cleaned up and stored away or given away to others. His clothing and books and so forth may be useful to other people. In that way your father can be helpful to others even after his death. In that way his death is not only about sadness but also about his helpfulness.

Be sure to get enough exercise. Avoid sitting for long periods staring at your father's photograph. By going on with your life, by doing your best, you are giving a special gift to your father. He would not be happy if you let grieving interfere with enjoying school and friends and other family members. So you can make your active life a meaningful memorial to your father.

If the feelings of sorrow continue to trouble you it is fine to see a school counselor or psychotherapist or physician. There are methods for handling depression, including medication. Remember that medicine may help with overwhelming feelings, but medicine doesn't tell you how to live. The way you live your life is up to you. Do your best, for yourself and for the memory of your father.

Question 9: I do lots of favors for my best friend, but he never thanks me. He never does anything for me. How can I get him to appreciate all I do for him?

You believe that you give more to your friend than you receive from him. My guess is that your friend believes that he gives more to you than he receives from you. We like to think we are givers and not takers. We quickly forget what we receive from others and remember for a long time what we do for them. In the same way we quickly forget the troubles we cause others, but we remember for a long time the troubles they cause us.

So I have a suggestion for you. Please look carefully at the favors you receive from your best friend. Be sure to thank him every time you notice his favors to you. You will become a model of noticing favors and thanking your friend for them. Your friend may notice the change in your behavior. He may begin to imitate you, thanking you for the favors you do for him. Anyway, as you develop your appreciation for your friend's kindness to you, the question about his appreciation of you will not be so important to you.

Question 10: I have a boyfriend, but recently I found someone I like more than him. How can I leave my current boyfriend smoothly so that I can have a new boyfriend?

It is hard to break up with a boyfriend or girlfriend. You want to be liked and respected by others, even after you move on to someone else. The important thing is to be honest and take responsibility for your actions. Make it clear to your boyfriend that he is fine as he is, but you need to explore a relationship with someone else. Be sure to thank your boyfriend for specific things he did for you while you were going together. Other girls, too, would appreciate the kindness he showed to you. Apologize for your selfish decision and firmly move along toward your new boyfriend.

Whether you return the gifts you received from the former boyfriend is up to you. And whether you are successful with your new boyfriend is up to you and the new boyfriend. Whenever possible it is best to keep former boyfriends as friends rather than enemies. You may feel relief and happiness or jealousy and regret when you see your former boyfriend with other girls. Whatever feelings appear in your mind go on with your life, doing the best that you can.

Question 11: My friend has an embarrassing habit of spitting on sidewalks and train platforms, anywhere. How can I tell him to stop without hurting his feelings?

We don't like to hurt other people's feelings or make them angry. Nevertheless, sometimes we must give them helpful information, even when the information is criticism. There are ways to make the criticism lighter, easier to take. In this case one way is to criticize yourself for the same habit. For example, "I used to spit on the sidewalk, but my sister told me I should stop doing it because it is impolite and unsanitary. So I don't do it any more."

Another way is to make a joke about your friend's habit. "You just drowned an ant! Here is an empty paper coffee cup. Save the ants!" Yet another way is to tell a story about spitting in general (not your friend's spitting), either a distant tale about someone else or some scientific information about the unhealthy contents of spit. The key here is to try to make it easier for your friend to hear your message about his bad habit. His friendship is important to you. Your responsibility to inform him about his poor habit is important, too. His habit has public health consequences and consequences for his image in other people's eyes, too.

Question 12: Every time I talk to another boy my boyfriend becomes jealous. Everything I do seems to make my boyfriend angry. What should I do?

You boyfriend's jealousy is his problem, not yours. Jealousy comes from insecurity, not from love. True love wants the best for the loved one. Jealousy wants to possess another person to protect the weak self. Your boyfriend's attempts to control you show his focus on himself, on his own limits.

If you let your boyfriend manage your life it will shrink and shrink. You will feel like you are in prison. So you must assert your own strength and refuse to be dominated, or you should break up with your boyfriend. Your kind resistance will force him to look at himself or run away. If you continue to be dominated he won't change. So you are doing him a favor by standing strong.

Question 13: My father still thinks I am a child. He thinks I don't know anything about life. He doesn't respect my ideas. How can I change him?

No one can change other people directly. So you cannot force your father to change. You can change what you do and hope those changes will influence your father. So your job is to show your father actions that he will respect.

For example, is your room neat and clean? Are your shoes lined up carefully when you enter the house (in Japan)? Do you keep your promises to your parents? Do you dress carefully in a way acceptable to your father? Is your speech at home polite and proper? Such actions are important if you hope your father's attitude toward you will change.

Next I have a suggestion about changing your attitude toward your father. You seem to think that your problem is not getting what you want from your father. I suspect that you focus too much on receiving from your father. I suggest that you consider giving back to him. From your early childhood you have been receiving from him. His income helped to feed you and clothe you. Maybe he bought you gifts and took you on trips and played games with you. Maybe he apologized to others in the neighborhood when you caused trouble. You took for granted your father's kindness to you for many years. Now that you want to be seen as more like an adult it is time to work on your debt to your father. Thank him when he does something for you. Remind him of the times when you were a child and he was kind to you but you forgot to thank him. Let your father know that you notice and appreciate what he has already taught you about life. Finally, find ways to repay your father with small gifts and services to show him that you are thinking with more maturity. Your actions will help you and your father to come to better agreement on your level of maturity.

Question 14: My grandparents are boring. My parents want me to be kind to my grandparents

and to spend time with them. But my grandparents are very old, and we have nothing in common. What could we talk about? What could we do together?

You can learn a lot from your grandparents if you ask the right questions. When they were young like you their lives were so different. When they talk about their youth it is like listening to tales of history. In their youth they didn't have computers and DVD's and electronic games, but they can tell you about adventures that you never imagined. I asked my 90-year-old mother to record her memories of her youth. She surprised and delighted me with her detailed stories of the distant past, but she couldn't remember what she did the day before we talked.

Your grandparents may be able to teach you skills like handicrafts and fishing and gardening and cooking and making friends. They took many years to develop these skills. In the past American and Japanese people treasured the wisdom of elderly people. Now is your chance to benefit from the wisdom of the elderly.

Question 15: My friend borrowed money from a loan company and can't pay it back. Now I

am paying back his debt with my money. It will take months to pay off the debt little by little. Am I doing the right thing?

You must decide what is best for you to do. Here are some things to think about:

1. You are helping your friend by paying his debt.
2. You are hurting your friend by taking away his chance to pay his own debt. He may take his debts lightly, thinking someone else will pay his debts for him.
3. How is paying your friend's debts affecting your economic situation? Do you have enough money for your own needs?
4. How is paying your friend's debts affecting your relationship with him? Do you feel resentment? Does he feel dependent? Do your actions help or hurt your friendship?
5. What do others think about you and your friend's debt. Do your parents know about it? Do your other friends know about it?
6. Is there a way for your friend to begin to repay his own debt again?

Question 16: I failed to pass the examination to get into the school I wanted. Now I don't want to go to school at all. If I can't have the best

school I don't want any school.

I understand that you want the best. Wanting the best is not a problem. However, life doesn't always bring us what we want. Sometimes we are in a hurry but encounter red lights on the road. Sometimes we are ill. We may not have enough money to buy everything that we want exactly when we want it.

Sometimes what we think is best is not the best after all. You may discover that a second-choice school or a third-choice school is better for you. The important thing is to keep on challenging life even when you don't get what you want. Don't give up. If you give up you have no chance of winning life's game. So do your best even when you feel disappointed. Do your best for your own future, for your parents, for all the people who depend on you now and in the future. Show them all how to keep going on without giving up.

Question 17: My body has an ugly shape and my hair is ugly and I wear ugly glasses. How can anybody like me?

Ideas about physical beauty change from country to country and from time to time. The women in 17th Century European paintings may not look beautiful to you today. Perhaps you don't look like a modern movie star. Many young women in the United States and in Japan are very sensitive about their looks and the shape of their bodies. Some young women worry about their appearance even though they look just fine. A few young women harm their faces and bodies with extreme efforts to look better.

As you grow older you will learn that when you love someone he or she doesn't look ugly to you. My guess is that your mother looks fine to you because you love her. You can make yourself look better by choosing nice clothes and good makeup and keeping your body healthy with good food and exercise. Don't forget that making yourself beautiful inside is important, too. By being kind and thoughtful and polite and dependable you can make yourself more loveable. When others love you then you will look just fine to them. You don't need friends who look only at the outside. You want friends who care about qualities of good character, not just good looks. Friends who are good and kind and dependable are important because we become like our friends, we begin to act like them and think like them. So it is important to choose friends who are beautiful inside.

Question 18: I have some unusual habits. For example, I like to study at home in my room wearing pajamas. And I like to eat spaghetti with grape jelly on it. What if people find out about my weird habits?

You might be surprised at the weird habits other people have. We tend to hide our unusual behaviors. We fear others might think we are strange. The habits you mentioned don't hurt anyone. They are fine.

If an unusual habit is discovered there are a few things you can do. Ask the discovering person if he or she has secret habits, too. They may not answer you, but they will remember that everyone has some hidden habits. Another thing you can do is make a joke about the habit. Laughing at yourself helps to ease the discomfort you feel. Furthermore, it lightens the topic for others, too.

There is a reason why you have each habit. The reason may be unusual, but it makes sense from your perspective. For example, jelly may taste good to you on spaghetti. Letting others know the reasons behind your habits helps make the habits seem less strange.

Please understand that you don't have to be exactly like everyone else. In the U.S.A., in Japan, or anywhere, the safest course is to appear to be just like everyone else. But that safe course may not be the most interesting course. It is just fine to have some different habits for good reasons. Enjoy your spaghetti!

Question 19: My mother and father don't seem to love each other. Did they ever love each other? How can I help them find love again?

We want our parents to be happy. We wish for them the best lives possible. Let's think about love. There are many kinds of love. One kind is the romantic love we see in movies and on television. Romantic love has tender words and kisses and sparkling eyes. Another kind of love is trusting love. Trusting love comes from years of living together, facing problems together, depending on each other in good times and difficult times. Romantic love is easy to see. You may have to look harder to see trusting love. Maybe your parents have trusting love. Signs of trusting love are words of thanks, smiles, and thinking about the convenience of each other.

Some parents are so busy that they think there is no time for love. Some parents think that love is only for younger people. We cannot change our parents' views about love directly. However, we can show them by our actions--by smiles and words of thanks and dependability and hugs--the love we feel for them. Our loving behavior may inspire them to feel more love for each other. When you see them showing more love and kindness to each other be sure to praise them and thank them and tell them how important their actions are. Remember, no one can turn feelings on and off just by wishing; yet everyone can behave in helpful ways no matter what they are feeling. We have more control in our lives when we focus on our behavior without fighting against our feelings.

Question 20: I feel tired all the time. I went to the doctor but there seems to be nothing wrong with my physical health. I sleep all the time; I don't want to get out of bed. I've been like this for three or four months now. I have no interest in anything. What is wrong with me?

It is important to check your physical health. If doctors can find no physical illness then it is possible that you have a psychological problem, perhaps depression. Are you avoiding something important by sleeping? Do you have good reasons for getting up? It is easier to get up in the morning when you have something pleasant ahead of you that day.

Let's start by listing some of the things you want to do. Are there places you want to go? Are there people you want to see? Is there special food you want to eat? Try getting out of bed for thirty minutes. Move your body. Take a walk. Then reward yourself with a favorite snack or some other reward. After thirty minutes you can go back to bed, but my guess is that you won't need to climb back into bed. Once you are up and moving about, the problem of getting up is solved.

In the morning wash and comb your hair and put on good clothes. Walk out of your home to a place where you can be with other people, with friends or relatives perhaps. Listen to their talk. Join in the conversation if you like. You may forget the time when you are involved in these group activities.

Little by little increase the time you are out of your bed and out of your room. Aim to be out of your room for at least eight hours every day. Your body will adjust to the change. Sometimes you may feel tired. You may want to retreat back to your bed at times. Feelings are natural; they come and they go. Don't let feelings govern your life. While feeling tired you can walk. While feeling shy you can listen to others and talk to them. Don't waste your life lying in bed more than eight hours a day for sleeping. Take charge of your behavior, and build an active life.

Question 21: My boyfriend wants to have sex. But we aren't married and I don't love him. He says everybody has sex. He says that he may choose another girlfriend if I don't sleep with him. What should I do?

The simple answer is find a better boyfriend, one who cares about what you want, too. Your current boyfriend selfishly wants to control you so he can satisfy his sexual urges. When someone genuinely loves you he will want to do what is best for you.

Sexual desires are natural and normal. But the finest people don't let sexual desires push them around. Whatever desires we feel, we are responsible for what we do. You can find other ways to show affection until you are ready to behave sexually. When you find someone to share time and conversations and interests you have found a true boyfriend.

Question 22: My parents try to choose my friends and my hobbies and my clothes and everything else for me. How can I get them to trust my judgment more?

Let your parents know that you appreciate their interest in your life. It is just that they are not showing their interest in the best way. One way to help them find other ways to show how much they care about you is to give them more choices. For example, show them several kinds of clothes you might wear today. All the clothes you suggest are acceptable to you. Then let them choose among the ones you suggested. You already have some idea about which clothes they will select. So they are now cooperating with you instead of fighting over what you will wear. If you are clever with your choices your parents will begin to see that you are choosing well, and they will begin to trust your judgment more.

Another way is to discuss with your parents the reasons for their preferences. Why do they dislike a certain friend of yours? Why do they prefer certain hobbies for you? Instead of flatly disagreeing it is wiser to find out what lies underneath their preferences. You become a kind of family detective seeking out some neutral ground for agreement. Your parents will trust your judgment more when they see you searching for reasons rather than just arguing for your point of view.

You know that time is on your side; so don't be in a hurry. As you grow older you will earn more independence as long as your behavior shows you deserve it.

Question 23: I want a car. I am old enough to drive and to own a car. I will take good care of one. But my parents won't buy me one. What should I do?

Here again we want to aim for cooperation instead of conflict. Find out what lies behind your parents' resistance. Is it financial? Can you do something about that? Is it your age and your behavior? Can you show them behavior that will change their perspective on your ability to be a trustworthy driver? Perhaps taking responsibility for cleaning the family car and other family chores will show your ability. Perhaps you can study to prepare for the driving test to show your readiness to obey the law. Perhaps your parents will allow you to get a learning permit that allows beginning progress such as parking practice and driving practice in safe environments. Perhaps you can find some way to pay for your future gasoline.

Notice that I suggest things you can do to change things. You cannot directly control your parents or anyone else. Work first to behave in ways that might change your parents' decisions. You can control your own behavior, no matter what you are feeling.

Question 24: My brother tells lies. He makes appointments then he doesn't keep them. I can't trust him. What can I do about him?

Although we can't control other people, we can try to influence them. One way to influence them is to reward them when they do what we want and ignore and avoid them when they don't. For example, when your brother makes an appointment and keeps it you can praise him or give him something he likes. When he lies you can tell him you don't like what he is doing and turn away and ignore him. Be sure that you are a good model for your brother by keeping your appointments and avoiding lies.

Question 25: I'm a young woman twenty-two years old. I'm looking for work now. I want to take my time and search carefully for a fine job. However my mother expects me to find a job quickly. Yesterday my mother was very irritated with me. How can I deal with her impatience?

As you know from experience, you cannot control your mother's impatience. You cannot turn her impatience on and off as you wish. To help her understand your plans you can discuss them with her. Tell her each day how your search for a job is progressing. You could set a limit on the time of your search. For example, you could tell your mother that you will certainly apply for a job within six months or three months.

Of course, it is your responsibility to search for a job every day. Searching for a job *is* your current job. On weekdays you should get up every morning and dress as though you were going to work. You should leave the house early to research information about jobs. You shouldn't return to your house until after 5 p.m. Looking for a job is sometimes the hardest job. I wish you good luck.

Question 26: I'm a young man of twenty-four living at home. My father is very strict with me. I wear a T-shirt with a golden necklace. My father doesn't like me to wear a necklace because I'm a male. My friends wear accessories, even earrings. How can I make my father understand without becoming angry?

In America it is not so common for a young man of your age to be living at home. Many Americans think that when young people live at home they must accept the rules of their parents. So many American young people live in an apartment or college dormitory when they are in their twenties. Living separately from their parents they have more freedom.

Perhaps you have economic or other reasons for living at home. Are you working? Are you a college student? Anyway, now you are enjoying the benefits of living at home. Someone prepares your meals, someone washes your clothes, and someone pays for your bedroom. While at home you have some responsibility to adapt to your father's wishes. Can you make a compromise with your father? For example, when you are at home you won't wear the necklace, but when you go out with your friends you will wear it.   Life is a combination of benefits and responsibilities. We cannot demand benefits only, without responsibilities. We cannot think about our own convenience and ignore the convenience of others. With the compromise described above both you and your father gain some benefits. Can you think of some other compromise that might satisfy both the young man and his father?

About the author

David K. Reynolds, Ph.D. served on the faculty of the UCLA School of Public Health, the USC School of Medicine, and the University of Houston. He is currently Director of the Constructive Living Center in Coos Bay, Oregon. He is the author of *Playing Ball on Running Water, Reflections on the Tao te Ching, Plunging Through the Clouds, A Handbook for Constructive Living* and more than twenty-five other books published in the United States, England, Germany, Australia, Japan, and China by university publishers and popular publishers. He began research in Japan in 1964 and continues to live in Japan for months each year. Dr. Reynolds is the only Westerner to have received the Kora Prize and the Morita Prize from the Japanese Morita Psychotherapy Association.

Contact at:

P.O. Box 85
Coos Bay, OR
97420
USA
Tel: 541-269-5591

and

13-27-102 Hon-cho Sakado-shi
Saitama-ken Japan 350-0226
Tel: 0492-81-1258

and

dkreynoldsjapan@gmail.com
http://docl.jp
http://constructiveliving2.weebly.com

Made in the USA
Middletown, DE
17 June 2023

32774225R00024